Meraki: Love Letters to Language

Μεράκι (May-rah-kee)
(adj.) describes doing something with creativity or
putting something of yourself into your work.

Written & illustrated by Elise Maren

Foreword

As poets, we find meaning in the miniscule and sometimes neglected details in life. For it is with these details that we can string together moments that move people emotionally and transport them into a moment that we have intentionally crafted.

The moment I met Elise, she immediately found it fascinating that I had released a collection of poetry and had a second on the way. She mentioned that she was in the process of penning *Meraki* and asked if I could write the foreword. Naturally I couldn't turn this opportunity down.

Reading *Meraki* gives you a glimpse into what it's like to slow down to fully feel love, get hurt by it, question it, and extend it to others. Her power lies in her impactful simplicity. She makes every word count in each of her poems. She covers a variety of emotionally intense topics laced with carefully placed humor that makes you chuckle. Yet, there remains space to fully absorb what the poem calls you to feel. Her ability to capture a variety of feelings parallel to love lies not restricted to sonnets, but in a wide variety of poetical forms. However, she showcases her mastery of villanelles in this collection.

Now it is time to search your cupboard for a mug that will do, sift through the teabags in your drawer, and get ready to enter moments of love that will move you at the core.

- Carlos Fernandes II

Preface

English stinks. I love to write in English mostly because it stinks. Bullying English by exploiting its grammar, homonyms, and numerous other peculiarities can make for amusing poetry. However, I find the language to have one unforgivable flaw: there is only one word for the notion of love. While Sanskrit boasts 96 words for love, we use one measly, catch-all term to describe feelings towards coffee, family, partners, and strangers alike.

When I was trying to come up with a way to categorize poems written from age fifteen to the present, the only thing I could come up with was to organize themes in terms of what type of love they convey. The Greek language facilitated this, and a book with Greek chapters needs a Greek title. From there, *Meraki: Love Letters to Language* was born. The title came quite naturally, as I have poured much of myself into this work. The subject sections include self-love, fondness, flirtation, desire, enduring love, familial love, love for humanity, lament, and hospitality. The themes vary widely: nature, queerness, spirituality, community, grief, and more.

As you'll see throughout *Meraki*, I find language generally fascinating. However, don't mistake me for a polyglot. It's all Greek to me – pun intended. You'll find poems that draw inspiration from Greek, Hebrew, Spanish, Hmong, Somali, Norwegian, Japanese, French, Cree, and Northern Sámi. Many thanks to the native speakers who helped me verify translations and concepts. Some poems are fully in another language and then translated into English on the next page. One poem in this book is only in English but is nearly unrecognizable; it uses obsolete vocabulary to tell a story about someone who reads the dictionary as she falls hopelessly in love with a librarian. Don't worry, I provided a glossary on the next page.

At the end of the book, you'll find an appendix providing further information and context about each poem if you'd like to learn more or did not catch a reference. I'm always curious what writers were thinking while they wrote, so I provided a bit of the behind the scenes for you. I aim to write the kinds of books I'd want to read.

Meraki is simultaneously a love letter to language and hate mail addressed specifically to English's rusty, old mailbox. I hope you enjoy reading *Meraki* just as much as I enjoyed creating it.

Table of Contents

Appendix
Preview of *The Periodical*

Φιλαυτία

(phil-auh-ti-ah)

to love oneself, or hold regard
for one's own happiness

Ode to Obscured Ancestors

Some may say you are no matter
As if you did not leave these delicate traces of fjords under my eyes.
The dips and valleys carved into my skin.
I am asked why I appear so weary, yet I remain proud.

Perhaps they result from miles traveled each day:
Footsteps of a nomadic life lost.
The most I'll run is around the lake,
But I store more endurance within.

I hail all strength from my fragile grandmother.
She had twig arms with a rugged Norse demeanor,
Eyes brighter than the aurora,
And a smile that cracked like lightning.

A loud connection between generations
Despite little to no depiction of our history.
Yet, with every breath of my harmonic prayers,
I sway to your stories in song.

Gudnejahttit Máttut Sii Čiegadedje

(*Ode to Obscured Ancestors* translated to the language of those ancestors: Northern Sámi)

Gii nu olmmošjoavku muitala mu don it dehálaš,
Gii jus du it bijat gurra eret rašši vuotna vuollel mu oaidnit.
Fávllimus ja vággi čuollat sisa mu náhkki.
Jearaha manne mun váikkuhit de váiban, muhto mun lean
čevllohallat.

Soaitit diet boađus eret gilomehter reaisu mátkkoštit juohke beaivi:
Juolgi luodda genitiv nomádaoahppu vahát.
Eanemus mun sáhtan golihit leat birra det jávri,
Muhto mun doalan eanet sávrodat siskkobealde.

Čuorpmastit visot vuoibmi eret mu rašši áhkku:
Oavssáš vearju mielde muhtun norrøna láhttenvuohki,
Čalbmi čuovgat gii avrá,
Ja muhtun modji gii álddagas.

Allat oktavuohta gaskal logijahki
Beroškeahttá eret unnán govvideapmi eret
iežame muitalus.
Ain mielde juohke vuoiŋŋanas eret mu
harmonalaš rohkos,
Mun heailu mielde du muitalus illativ lávlla.

A Primer for Eluding Death by Cave Dweller

A four-part Duplex-style poem engaging with the process of 'enlightenment' from the perspective of a prisoner in Plato's infamous *Allegory of the Cave*.

Εἰκασία (Conjecture)

What is life beyond the dim light?
The fine gray scale of a bird's wing?

> I know the laughter of a bird's wing.
> It mocks like the prisoner next to me.

Stuck like the prisoners next to me.
They do not believe they are imprisoned.

> I know that we were imprisoned.
> Each day I whittled away at my freedom.

One day I skittered away with my freedom,
Rising from plight as I broke from chains.

> Breaking towards light as I rose from chains,
> I saw my shadow there staring back at me.

Like my shadow, is there form to a bird?
I believe in life beyond the dim light.

Πίστις (Belief)

I believe in life beyond the dim light.
Life flashed before my eyes in an all-consuming fire.

> Shapes of life danced before an all-presuming fire,
> Where bodies laughed like birds, holding them high.

Each bird was held just above a wall so high;
Bodies cackled and shuffled out of my sight.

> Fire crackled and muffled as I shifted my sight,
> And drifted with scorn around the cave.

Now that I know I was born in a cave,

I am certain there is more than flat form.

Stubborn enough to follow the Earth's form,
I finally wandered into the blinding sun.

Engulfed in wonder by the spellbinding sun,
I have seen life beyond the dim light.

Διάνοια (Intellect)

I have seen life beyond the dim light,
Where birds sing to the beat of technicolor wings.

Stinging my eyes to greet the true colors of things,
I cannot help but think that this life is complete.

I think the lives of the other dwellers are not complete.
How joyful they would be to see a *real* bird!

Or would they laugh like a crafted bird?
And consider me to be flightier than the stick!

I worry they might try to put me on the stick.
Is enlightenment about spite or duty?

Now that I know the sky, is it delight or duty
To bring this knowledge back into the cave?

Although I begin my descent back into the cave,
I blissfully rise to reason beyond the dim light.

Νόησις (Understanding)

I regrettably rose to reason beyond the dim light.
When dealing with the dogmatic, try to remain Socratic.

No matter how pragmatic your reasons are.
No matter how systematic your ideas are.

Things will get erratic if you act like a fanatic.
Each day I silently watch hints drop like flies.

Each day I watch memories drop like flies.
Fond impressions of the sun fade into mere forms.

Fellow dwellers cannot conceive beyond mere forms.
Their words burned as I tried to put out the fire.

      Even breathing felt like putting out a fire,
      Although I always took heed while they fought.

I will never concede although they plot
My demise to be treason against the dim light.

The Perennial Purpose

Biologists classify leaves by their features,
Textures, shapes, placements, and uses.
Certainly, it is valuable to notice how
Palm fronds heal bodies,
Waxy pine needles yield resilience,
And respite is found in the shade of a sturdy oak.
Yet, when we focus on utility,
We miss the forest for the trees.

May we praise a leaf for its pliancy.
Simply by respiring, it might
Bear fruit,
Breathe life into others,
And watch water roll off its
back.
Existence is growth,
So what say humanity?

Lay in the sun.
Bask in your inherent worth.
Weep with the willows.
Rest your head beneath the
dogwood tree.
What must die for us to
bloom?
As death rears life,
So what say you?

In Another Time

100 years of queer history inspired by the ending line from Sappho.

Masquerading identities by hiding in Harlem.
Tell them we're anything but a drag.
Prohibition, admission, recognition.
Speakeasy, honey.

The glitter lasts until next June: devil's dandruff and craft herpes.
Rainbow banners on windows: pink triangles and shudders.
Alan Turing, terming, turning,
Toward an era where love is the cure, not the illness.
Unsightly, virtually off the GRID.
Disorder is only present when we demonstrate.

Kinsey, kindsey, kindly found a prism to make our spectrum
visible.
How many times must we ACT UP?
Laws are adopted while our children are not.
Demonstrate, second-rate, second-class.
Anything but criminal.

Loosen me from blunt agony.
Each of us already fighting at least two wars.
Sir, ma'am, captain.
Don't ask, don't tell.

It's been four years, but we can still feel the Pulse of our siblings.
Today we march the same as
Marsha P., marshal peace, march and pay them no mind.
They place bricks to place blame as we hold our heads up with
pride.

You may forget but
Someone, I tell you, will remember us,
Even in another time.

Battlefield
A moment in the life of someone with audio-color synesthesia.

Cubist-era machine guns of cobalt blues bombard
my ears with clicking as my feet shuffle into the room
with a sherbet shade of orange.
Focus.

Students of all shapes and colors reside in painfully
similar plastic chairs with their hands flying over sheets
of keys and neoprene.
Focus.

Some sit quietly. Some sing of whispered sunshine and
violets. Some snark away in drab smagdarine.
Focus.

I find my place between a girl who speaks in exquisite
fretworks of crimson, and a boy who yammers and
gabs in iterations of lime green.
FOCUS.

Placing my hands along a brigade of graphemes,
I begin to barrel away and find a steady flow of focus.

The crusade of color subsides.

Kairos | καιρός

Ancient Greek word for a critical or opportune moment.
Modern Greek word for weather.

Do you remember the night when
The lightning struck and purple poured across the sky,
But it was gone before you could even blink?
The rain poured down in polka dots of waterfalls
And the mud squished between my toes.
And all at once.
The thunder clapped.
The rain fell.
The branches snapped.
And the lightning struck my mind.
So that's when I knew
Exactly how to feel.

I want to be struck by lightning
Just to feel the current in my
hands.

φιλία

(phil-ee-ah)

affectionate regard,
friendship between equals

Buorre beaivvi, Hnub Ci

"Morning ____!
My name is Elise
And I'll do your OCT
Before you see
The doctor. Just
A quick picture of
The back of your eyes."

My friend Nouchi
Is at the front
Desk. Her name means
Sunshine. I am blessed
To be from a place where
We have the largest
Populations outside
Our ancestral
Homelands.

"Buorre beaivvi!
Mun lean Elise
Ja aigut dahkat du OCT
Ovdalgo don oaidnit.
Dat doavttir. En
A johtilit govva
Dat du čalmmi."

What I said means
"Good sun!
I am Elise."
Not "My name is."
We declare
Who We are.
My people respond
With *"Ipmel atti!"*
"The Universe
Has given it
To Us."

happy valentines day, my friend! xoxo norche

Mun lean Sapmelaš. I am Sámi.

Mitakuye owas'in. We are all relatives.

Vessels

Shall I compare us to a glass pitcher?
The crack in the bottom will make empty.
What fills up the pitcher makes life richer.
Surrounded by love means we have plenty.

Humans are a vessel, not a houseboat.
We cannot live solely in others' dreams.
The word empty should not be all she wrote.
Lives are not often as good as it seems.

Others' emotions I will not wrestle.
Joy and suffering we cannot predict.
I am an abundant, finite vessel.
Filling up buckets before they are kicked.

      In minds we cannot have people reside,
      But with love, hand in hand, we will abide.

The Cedar

The *mâsikisk* hung above my door frame:
A gift of peace from a friend when I was sick.
He prayed over tobacco and sage without shame
And we released the ashes into the crick.

In a glorious revival of childhoods,
We learned from each other's traditions.
Even on our cold walks into collegiate woods,
It felt warm to be loved without conditions.

Letter to an Old Dog

At age eight I made a PowerPoint,
To convince my mom to get a dog like you.
To my dismay, all they did was anoint
Me as the dog sitter, new.

Your family dropped you off before their vacation
With a basket of toys, food, and leashes for walks.
Although you were not mine, to my elation
We found that you loved to steal my brother's socks.

By taking you in each time a trip would arise,
Your personality changed my mom's mood.
When I was sixteen, to my surprise,
To a puppy you became the prelude.

Now I find you at sixteen years old
With rickety joints and charming gray ears.
In training old dogs, you made me bold.
Cheers to all your joyful years.

The Bus from Abingdon

My new apartment hallway has the same
Old, weird plastic smell that yours did.
It smells like walking inside and losing the
Homesickness-induing ability
To see my bated breath.

But, it rarely gets that cold in Oxford.
God's got to keep Her precious books
Warm somehow. I was there when I
Learned that God is a woman too.
She loves with abandon,
Never to abandon.

You don't believe in the same
God, but we both believe in
The truths of the world
That good science brings.

Weeds on the Playground

As weeds eclipse the playground,
We find ourselves at twenty-three.
Years from counting bugs found,
Today we entertain ourselves with tea.

We find ourselves at twenty-three.
Reminiscent of spirits who felt more free.
Today we entertain ourselves with tea.
Children at heart we may be.

Reminiscent of spirits who felt more free.
Years from counting bugs found,
Children at heart we may be.
Yet, weeds eclipse the playground.

Yoko Meshi | 横飯

(n.) the peculiar stress caused by speaking a foreign language.
literally, a meal eaten sideways.
chopsticks
and bowl
carved from
rosetta stone.

every fallen
grain of
rice
constructs
my own tower
of babel
under
the table.

an attempt
to speak
with anyone
else

is like
trying
to eat
sushi
and

see
the rice
spill
out one
side of
my
mouth.

よこメッシュ

ソノキモチワカル

Checkmate.
Check. My hands quiver.
New battery. Carefully calculated.
Touch base. Refresh. Revise.
This plan was naive. Stalemate.
My foot slips. En passant!
Steps. We start to ascend.
Moving them, envisioning our next
I begin with my four pawns on the ground;
For people who cannot sit still.
Rock climbing is just chess

Chess for Creatives

Søndag

Norwegian word for *Sunday* or the tradition of taking a nature walk
every Sunday.

Do you know that visceral feeling
Of wanting to hug any puppy you see?
Am I the only one who feels similarly
When I see a lake? I want to be consumed
By Her. I want to be reborn in her depths.

She is my church. I want to baptize the books
I've been beaten with, hang them out to dry,
And tear out the hateful pages. Then,
My siblings will not be beaten with the heaviest
Dogma and mistranslations colonizers can find.

I swim, immersed in Her all-consuming love.
I look upon the hill where conifers
Exclaim boldly amongst the
Chlorophyll exodus. When will I be free
Enough to maintain my color?

Ερωτοτροπία

(eroto-rope-ia)

flirtatious, puppy love

Wish You Were Here

I wish you were here
In the Land of 10,000 Lake Streets.
Soon, I'll be able to hold you near
And listen to Lake Michigan's heartbeats.

The Knowing

I want to know how you take your coffee,
Which mug you use, which hand, and why.
I won't judge you if it's sugary and frothy,
But I'll tease you each morning with a kiss goodbye.

I want to know why you don't love the sun.
Indoors or out, I lay in the rays like a dog.
Would you take me on a hike, even just one?
Trading the rays for woodland mist and fog.

I want to know what called you to heal.
I want to know what called you to teach.
I want to know how you're already making me feel
Something I thought was frankly out of reach.

Whirlpool

I'm sure she'll be a gentleman and cool.
On my love life I should not dwell.
I'm swimming laps in the dating pool.

Can't count the times I've been ghosted or ghouled;
Twisted energies I aim to repel.
But I'm sure she'll be a gentleman and cool.

Been used enough times to feel like a tool.
At least they prompt me to grab my inkwell.
I'm swimming laps in the dating pool.

Treading this water feels unusual and cruel.
At least I'll have some stories to tell!
I'm sure she'll be a gentleman and cool.

I don't have the money to buy her a jewel
But I'll comb the beach to find her a shell.
I'm swimming laps in the dating pool.

For poetry, I never went to school.
Avoiding similes like the plague, hell.
I'm sure she'll be a gentleman and cool.
I'm swimming laps in the dating pool.

Sonnet for my Local Drive-In

Left off Hudson Boulevard. Follow tracks.
Just cash. Ninety-point-one on stereo.
Backseats stacked with cozy blankets and snacks.
Midwest mosquitoes itching for a show.

Conversation so rich, hate to press pause
On your sharp mind; you use words like groovy!
Thank goodness others can't hear us because
We are the type to talk during the movie.

Surveying the sun, it bids us goodbye;
A swirling sorbet in sweltering June.
No painted craft of mine could match that sky,
But darling, I presume you hung the moon.

    Lightning bugs direct our way home through the pine,
    One hand on the wheel and one hand in mine.

Misplaced Redame

An ode to the concept of falling in love with the wrong librarian
and reading the dictionary as an excuse to hang out around her. See
next page for glossary.

I read the dictionary A-Z but still can't find the words
To tell an acquaintance that I love her, no matter how absurd.

>I would give you the world, of which ours is absurd.
>Of which can feel solivagant, for better or for worse.

Around you, gastric butterflies get worse.
I bring a packed lunch to avoid abligurition.

>If you're feeling artophagous, I'd take you for jentacular
abligurition.
>I'd cherish your matutinal radiance and smaragdine eyes.

I admittedly admire your eyes
When you read feminist and womanist theory.

>I hesitate to cachinnate when we canvass peristonic theory.
>A true sarcast you are, yelling stage whispers in a library.

I sit here, but I do not have a card for this library.
Steeped in this accismus with my anonymuncle murmurations.

>I painfully withhold opinionated murmurations
>With regards to your latest suitor.

Spanghew your barbatulous, hircine, psittaceous suitor;
His chatter is nonsense and it puts you in a sloom.

>When I daydream or have a sloom,
>I yearn for devotion in my anecdotage.

You would boast of my uxoriousness until our anecdotage,
But I cannot prefestinate in my scripturience.

>You make me feel scripturient,
>But I still can't find the words...

Glossary

Redame: to love in return

Solivagant: describes wandering alone

Gastric: relating to the stomach

Abligurition: lavish spending on food or drink

Artophagous: inclined to eat bread

Matutinal: occurring in the morning

Smaragdine: emerald green

Cachinnate: laugh loudly

Canvass: discussion of opinions on or raising awareness for a topic

Peristonic: relating to pigeons (here relating to the Birds Aren't Real conspiracy)

Sarcast: sarcastic person

Accismus: a form of irony in which a person feigns indifference or pretends to refuse something they desire

Anonymuncle: anonymous writing

Murmurations: the act of murmuring (or, interestingly enough, flocks of starlings)

Spanghew: to throw in the air, historically with regard to frogs...

Barbatulous: with unimpressive facial hair

Hircine: of or resembling a goat

Psittaceous: like a parrot

Sloom: light slumber

Anecdotage: old age

Uxoriousness: overt devotion to one's wife

Prefestinate: predestine or predict, to make too much haste

Analgesic for Growing Pains

Sally forth, darling.
Colorado was right on cue.
Rocky Mountains are tall enough
To stand between me and you.

Like berries from your garden,
It was too sweet to be true.
I know what you feared from
A form of friendship all too new.

Bound by an ethereal night
In your backyard feeling carefree.
Nervous hands tracked shooting stars,
And inscribed your books with tea.

In trouble with family for staying too late;
A bugless night they could not conceive.
You texted apologies for daring not
To arise in fear I would leave.

Last time I saw you was on the lake;
Your head rested on my thigh.
I swung the paddle around my back
To navigate and keep you dry.

I carried on blissfully in the sun
With fear the fling had flung.
I would do things differently but
Our opportunity has sprung.

I dream of your head on my chest,
And our novels held to the sky.
Somehow I focus best when you
Trace plotlines on my thigh.

That summer flew by so fast and
Next autumn, I'll fly north.
So dare I say, darling,
Sally forth.

Yesterday Morning

A cherished walk in the park:
Refreshing, should you match my pace.
On Socratic trails we embark
To charm our minds in each embrace.

Refreshing, should you match my pace.
Trading a quip for each remark
To charm our minds in each embrace.
A beloved, maddening spark.

Trading a quip for each remark.
Do understand why I should chase
A beloved, maddening spark
We try but know we can't replace.

Do understand why I should chase.
On Socratic trails we embark
We try but know we can't replace
A cherished walk in the park.

ἔρως
(eh-ros)

desire or intimate appreciation
of internal or external beauty

Green for Your Eyes

Green for your eyes.
Charm and kindness scintillate.
So deeply saturated color cries,
For this youth's passing I await.

Charm and kindness scintillate.
Preludes of ardor act as dawn and demise.
For this youth's passing I await,
And only to God I petition reprise.

Preludes of ardor act as dawn and demise.
We cannot dictate nature's fate,
And only to God I petition reprise
Of which I will bear the weight.

We cannot dictate nature's fate.
So deeply saturated color cries
Of which I will bear the weight
Of green for your eyes.

From Stardust

Something that cannot tip a scale
Lays heavy in a hand.
Your words discordant;
Hands still clenched tightly.
My mirror reflects like elegy for
An almost unrecognizable self.
For this, I am pleased.

Hebrew renders depth I never shared.
Ink lays more thick, weighty typewriters click,
Disoriented pigment curls and drips off pages.

Watercolors scream dissonant sharps.
Scintillating photons yield illusions of mass.
Even mourning light through the window is heavy today,
And from mouths, masses of letters periodically change.

Laughable orbits of the spheres serenade us with tragedies;
Gravitational waves of intimacy pull us tighter.
I fear I am simply interference.

Argon

A chemistry student falling for an astrophysicist.

Feeling like a wimp, I left there inert.
Is it noble to say nothing at all?
Sensing that it may be fruitless to flirt,
Perhaps I should have chatted to the wall.

Clearly crushed by my thoughts I am not free.
Do I want to be you or be with you?
I thought I should at least ask you to tea
And you giggled a yes as if on cue.

Rain insisted an ethereal peace
And each of your thoughts were dripping in prose.
I watched starry eyes and my breathing cease
As you counted the freckles on my nose.

Temporal constellations disappear
Iterating their stories until dawn.
Spirits remain high in this atmosphere,
Lamenting for the day these nights argon.

As we know only fools are satisfied,
I crave such conversations rarefied.

Calamitous Consonants

Every time I say your name,
Something sticks under my tongue.
It sticks and it stings.
It burns and it clings.
It's a beautiful song unsung.

Forming each letter, I start to cringe
And pray these stars align.
Calamitous consonants,
Can you hear them singe?

Will I ever call you mine?

Boulevard of Broken Pens

All I have is this makeshift broken pen bouquet
To give you along with my pathetic plea.
My trash can is full of crumpled cliché;
Heartbreak and writer's block I must decree.

Along with my pathetic plea,
I have arguments for you to weigh.
Heartbreak and writer's block I must decree.
I wish so deeply for you to stay.

I have arguments for you to weigh.
I would be surprised if we agree.
I wish so deeply for you to stay.
I need to let my ideas run free.

I would not be surprised if we agree;
My trash can is full of crumpled cliché.
I need to let my feelings run free,
But all I have is this broken pen bouquet.

πρᾶγμα
(prague-mah)

pragmatic, enduring, covenantal love

תֹאמֶר רוּת אַל־תִּפְגְּעִי־בִי לְעָזְבֵךְ
לָשׁוּב מֵאַחֲרַיִךְ כִּי אֶל־אֲשֶׁר תֵּלְכִי
אֵלֵךְ וּבַאֲשֶׁר תָּלִינִי אָלִין עַמֵּךְ
עַמִּי וֵאלֹהַיִךְ אֱלֹהָי:
בַּאֲשֶׁר תָּמוּתִי אָמוּת וְשָׁם
אֶקָּבֵר כֹּה יַעֲשֶׂה יְהוָה
לִי וְכֹה יוֹסִיף כִּי
הַמָּוֶת יַפְרִיד בֵּינִי וּבֵינֵךְ:
וַתֵּרֶא כִּי־מִתְאַמֶּצֶת הִיא לָלֶכֶת
אִתָּהּ וַתֶּחְדַּל לְדַבֵּר אֵלֶיהָ:

וַתֵּלַכְנָה שְׁתֵּיהֶם עַד־בּוֹאָנָה בֵּית לָחֶם וַיְהִי
כְּבוֹאָנָה בֵּית לֶחֶם וַתֵּהֹם כָּל־הָעִיר עֲלֵיהֶן וַתֹּאמַרְנָה הֲזֹאת נָעֳמִי:
תֹּאמֶר אֲלֵיהֶן אַל־תִּקְרֶאנָה לִי נָעֳמִי קְרֶאןָ
לִי מָרָא (א במקום ה) כִּי־הֵמַר שַׁדַּי לִי מְאֹד:

Rose Thorn Crowns

To know her is to leave violets at her door,
To hum love songs on the way home,
To dream of respected covenants.

To know him is to read with abandon,
To be delivered from strongholds,
To cling to widows, outcasts, and that which is good.

To know her is to wipe the tears from her face,
To hear him weep with us,
To water flowers with the cup that overflows.

To know him is to anoint his feet with our perfume,
To dance among the righteous in fields of green carnations,
To uplift faithful centurions amid their plights.

To know her is to braid rosebuds into her hair,
To write vows in years of tea on Sunday mornings,
To be fully understood through eyes filled with divine light.

To know him is to run to without sight,
To be embraced when earth deems you unclean,
To seek love and justice with reckless abandon.

Now in my heart I see clearly,
Two beautiful faces shining back on me
Stained with love.

Spring Cleaning

Recently I left the Sunshine Queen
To her own devices, trusting that
She will still shine her
Best Rays without me.

She taught me how
To shine brighter and
I departed with a
Rare sunburn of the
Soul. My translucent
White skin rarely burns
From roots in the Land of
The Midnight Sun.
Is that poetic?

I found him aside his
Paints amongst the
Tall grasses which
Call me home.

He takes the skeletons
In my closet out to brunch
Without fear. He dances
In my warm laundry filled
With clothes that represent
Me today and things that
Barely fit anymore.

In his care, I will
Shed my exoskeleton
And kindly excuse the
People, ideas, and items
I grew out of.

I want to be as laid back
As he is. He is like the
Juniper. Something is
In bloom.

U-Haul

After the second date, she moved into my car.
Her perfume lingered in there
And on my coat for a week.
She drove me places I've never been.

After the third date, she made herself
At home in my mind.
After my therapy, she said,
"I like what you've done with the place."

After one year, the receipt from
Our first date moved from my
Glove box into a frame above
The bed I sometimes share with her.

After two years, the stolen sweaters
Shared the same closet and the
Travel mugs stopped moving
Between homes like kids of divorce.

After three years, I chose a ring
Out of silver that will never
Tarnish like we will. Polishing
Is a habit that I shall commit to.

After sixty years, her face has
So many wrinkles that it looks
Like a roadmap to heaven, which
I pray to be teatime on the porch.

Feeling Wholly

A Lutheran-born Norski coming to terms with queerness,
and the fact that Norwegians can, in fact, discuss emotions.

Å snakke rett fra leveren i en fei,
Should I not say the quiet part out loud?
Jeg er stolt over å være glad i deg.

The holiness of a love some vilify.
To froward theology my head is unbowed.
Å snakke rett fra leveren i en fei.

Companionship like yours is hard to come by,
Wholly queer, feeling alone in a crowd.
Jeg er stolt over å være glad i deg.

Taught to think I was at most an ally,
Even though shame was cast away with the shroud.
Å snakke rett fra leveren i en fei.

With a wearing duty to testify,
Each exhale is prose of which to be proud.
Jeg er stolt over å være glad i deg.

Away from your heart I will never shy,
Nor from feelings of which I have freshly avowed.
Å snakke rett fra leveren i en fei,
Jeg er stolt over å være glad i deg.

Norski: A Norwegian-American.

Å snakke rett fra leveren i en fei: "To speak from the liver in one sweep," Norwegian idiom for speaking earnestly.

Jeg er stolt over å være glad i deg: "I am proud to be fond of you," a milder version of _"Jeg elsker deg,"_ the most rare and serious expression of love.

Froward: To be habitually disposed to opposition as if it were law. See Proverbs 8:13.

Shroud: Burial covering, here alluding to the death of Jesus.

A Joik for my Love

Joik: a traditional Sámi song meant to encapsulate a moment, a being, or a place.

Hey a la le lo lo na
My song flows through the knots in your hair.
The notes echo across your hips like mountain tops.
Hey a la le lo lo na
Nostalgic joiks make me feel like I am in a moment there.
Sacred songs make time feel like it stops.
Hey a la le lo lo na
I am honored to teach you my beloved prayer.
Now, can you hear joiks in the rain drops?
Nah nah ne lo no nah

Simultaneous

There is no better place for me to be
Than in times of need to stand by your side
When you exist at the same time as me.

Most moments with you contain pure glee,
But when on your shoulder I have cried,
There is no better place for me to be.

I love how you can name almost every tree.
I rejoice in the freedom to simply abide,
When you exist at the same time as me.

In your embrace I feel entirely free,
And I find it easy to put worries aside;
There is no better place for me to be.

You contain multitudes beyond your beauty.
I pray someday you'll be my bride,
When you exist at the same time as me.

On the sanctity of us, I think we agree.
For more time with you, I would bide.
There is no better place for me to be,
When you exist
at the same time as me.

First Lady

My lover knows First Lady facts.
She's never dated a woman,
But please explain her love for Jackie Onassis.

My lover teaches me how to cook,
And discusses black holes poignantly
Over homemade vats of spaghetti.

My lover can sing with any bird.
She identifies trees by their leaves,
And flowers by the petal.

Someday the trees will clap their hands
And the flowers' dew will weep,
As I commit to being her First Lady.

στοργή
(stor-gah)

familial love

Blood

Sometimes love is there for a daughter.
To close families I raise a toast,
But sometimes blood runs like water.

Children molded at the hands of the potter.
Parent and child growing ever close.
Sometimes love is there for a daughter.

Boiling blood runs eternally hotter,
Ever hallucinating seeing your ghost.
Sometimes blood runs like water.

Overprotection like hands of a spotter.
Benevolent like the heart of a host.
Sometimes love is there for a daughter.

Feeling betrayed like a lamb to the slaughter.
Humor these days growing ever morose.
Sometimes blood runs like water.

Holding hands just like the otter,
In either scenario we are fully engrossed.
Sometimes love is there for a daughter.
Sometimes blood runs like water.

Chosen

As the dim, familiar light continues to flicker,
Friends are chosen to watch you bloom.
The blood of the covenant is thicker
Than the water of the womb.

They Dance with Me

My mom can't cook
But she will feed the children's
Souls, minds, and bodies until
There is no crumb left in the pantry.

My dad can't sing like my brother
But he will sing your praises
Until the cows come home
To dance in your delights.

My mom can't braid like me
But she wove her knowledge
And her courage into
Every fiber of my being.

My dad can't wear sunscreen.
Surprisingly he isn't a lobster,
But he does get crabby when
I throw sunscreen from the shade.

My mom can't ask for help.
She is the reason I look for
women with strong boundaries
Instead of broad shoulders.

My dad can't argue easily.
He is not the reason that
I, too, sometimes bark
at good-hearted men.

My mom can't dance,
But she dances with me
To the music she was raised on
While she is learning to cook.

The Lightest Reindeer calf

Voluminous snowflakes fell on my icy face and immediately dispersed into raindrops, which ran like soft, joyful tears upon the sight of the *čuoivvatmiessi*, the lightest and littlest reindeer calf. I, too, was feeling somehow lost yet also found by her company in the vast Norwegian wood. How long had she been searching for her herd? How long did it take me to get here to find a warmth in new people that felt like family, like home? It took me nearly twenty years.

We left nothing but footprints and hoofprints in the *njáhtso*, or wet snow, as we sauntered toward the sight of soft smoke. The *lávvu*, an elaborate, conical tent concealing a crackling fire, approached us with the offering of her herd.

Warm stew, cloudberries, and hugs greeted me at the entrance of the *lávvu* to kick off a night of songs and stories with people that treated me like *sohka*, extended family.

ἀγάπη
(ah-gahp-peh)

charity, love for humanity, or Divine love

Liturgy of the Ordinary

Every glorious morning, I greet
The hidden poets beneath my feet.
The moss, the bugs, and the rocks below
Write elegant sonnets for only them to know.

Tell people in the elevator you like their shoes
Litter compliments; there is nothing to lose
Drop all the worries and weights you carry
And delight in the liturgy of the ordinary.

Thank the janitor for their devotion
To be someone we rely on in all the commotion
Of the bustle of life. We all chip in
To the community, but rarely look within.

Too many sweet moments are wrongfully ignored.
Dance along to the taps of your keyboard.
Relish the crisp scents of flowers and rain.
Revere the holiness of the mundane.

One day I will join in the poets' song,
Starting ten feet down
Where my shell will belong.
From stardust we were made,
Each being an equal.
May we embrace every step
Made towards the sequel.

She Sings

Egg flips keep time to guitar strings.
Teapots pouring love, breaking fasts.
And of such mercies, morning sings.

Dogwood displays warring of kings;
A kiss to expel red contrasts.
Human hands, to the cross He brings.

The whistling spring wind softly stings.
Søndag stops time, His grace ever lasts.
And of such mercies, morning sings.

Our Mother's weeping body clings,
Tight to kin, never outcasts.
Human hands, to the cross He brings.

Her sonorous voice tunelessly rings
Bursting with joy, despite our pasts.
And of such mercies, morning sings.

Rising from sin, such glorious things.
All blood poured out and no stain lasts.
Human hands, to the cross He brings,
And of such mercies, morning sings.

Helium

The glee of a ten-year-old's days.
The itch of a corduroy chaise.
The flicker and glitch of technicolor
rich,
Upon which her eyes lay agaze.

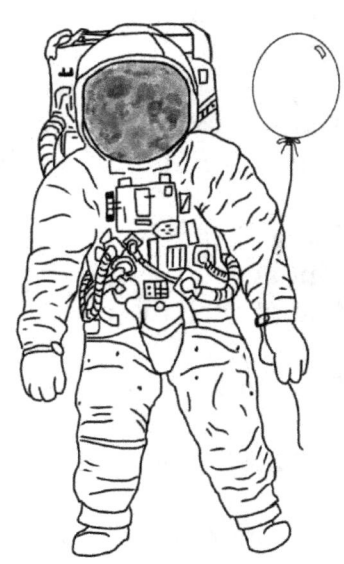

In their success she would wallow.
In their footsteps she should follow.
She let out a cheer, for in one short
year,
She'd have something in common
with Apollo.

For there was no doubt in her mind,
The same zeal for stars she'd find
In Double Dutch leaps, schooling for
keeps,
And her own small steps to be kind.

Who'd have thought that little Louise
Would muse physics as the bee's knees?
Despite her pride, they could not hide
Dispositions steeped in unease.

"Don't get me wrong, I believe you can fly!
Like your birthday balloon in this searing July."

Her grandpa let out a sigh…
For he was one heck of a guy
Who walked with a limp, dreamt of helium blimps,
And whispered with a tear in his eye,

"I don't suspect I'll find peace of mind
'til a gal like you holds a piece of the sky."

Gentile

Welcome is an empty word.
I am aware you don't want me here.

Yet,
All holy places endure invasions wholly.
There is no need to be gentile
As the divine occupies flesh
And a donkey descends upon a manger.
How dare human arrogance make inroads upon where we stand?

So gather, luxuriant graces and beautiful-haired muses.
For there is no dance, no holy place, from which we are absent.

Sounds of Rounds with the Patient Care Philharmonic

This music breathes an obstetric flute prelude,
And piccolos pair to the screeching etude.
A surgeon raises a PICC, lute precision bound.
Until discharge, nurses carry the tune round.
The family heads home in a hopeful mood.

The bowed head of the neurologist did conclude
Upon need for an anesthetic interlude.
In recovery, his treasured snore will resound.
This music breathes.

When the dermatologic fiddler viewed
How the rays from his days in the sun accrued,
She unleashed the emergency banjo sound.
In heading home, poignant reflection is found.
Even when beats of malleative care cue finitude,
This music breathes.

The Blessing of the Sun, the River, and the Moon

To be blessed
Is to have the sun
Kiss your skin
And for you to absorb
The light so that
You may radiate
Onto others.

To be blessed
Is to have the river
Wash over you with
The deepest love.
You may be baptized
In Her depths
And anointed with
Liveliness.

To be blessed
Is to have the moon
Shine down on you
In your darkest hour.
To see God and creation
In the mosaic of
Constellation.
May you rest knowing
That you are merely
Beloved stardust.

My Sister, Mary Oliver

The nurse addressed my five-year-old self, "Are you excited to have a baby brother?"
I retorted, "I am having either a sister or a puppy." I grew up to adore my brother and consider him a close friend, but thank God for Mary.

Mary was the sister I never had. She was small enough to fit in my purse, but vast enough to consume a mind for hours, if not days, on end. I remember when we went Home for the first time. I held her hand as we waltzed the same fjords as my ancestors. The October wind bit our skin like the mosquitoes we left behind but cozying up next to a fire under reindeer pelts healed both the bumps and the lumps in our throats from things unexplained and unexamined.

I want to be like the birch tree: afraid of nothing, especially not the depths of the sea or the heights of the sky. She jets high into the blue arctic oasis as if she cannot fathom the ground. The orange leaves are sprinkled across the peat and around my head, complimenting the blue hue. My hat is white like the snowcaps, but I cannot stand quite as tall. The trail waves to us. The brook babbles thoughts that make more sense than anything I have ever heard. The mist blurs my view, but I am content, nonetheless.

The aurora dances better than anyone I have ever known, and I have been to South America. She is mesmerizing in blue and green. Now I believe in love at first sight.

Do you know that visceral feeling of wanting to hug any puppy you see? Am I the only one who feels similarly when I see a body of water? I want to be consumed by her. I want to be reborn in her depths.

The Nomadic Ways of Wildflowers and Weeds

The chorus of chokecherry coughs, thimbleweed breaths, and ragweed sneezes echo across the meadow. Rattlesnake ferns kiss ankles in the grass, and the benevolence of the smooth serviceberry bows to the wind. The wallflower listens with intent.

Field mustard colonizes the grass, uprooting the wildflowers and edging them out of the meadow. Invasive yellow flowers radiate like the sun until plucked from the land. After a long day of tending the meadow, lay in the fragrant bedstraw until it, too, loses its place as a nosy neighbor.

Tiptoe around the touch-me-not, pet the labrador, and honk at the gooseberry. Rinse your face with kinnickinnick dewberry and bask in the silliness of your surroundings.

Third Fig
An expansion of Edna St. Vincent Millay's *First Fig* and *Second Fig*

When it appears we have all met our ends
Is it easier to drown or to thirst?
But ah, my foes, and oh, my friends–
Tis' no greater vict'ry than the first!

fig. 1

Θρήνος
(three-nohs)

lament

Longing for a New Moon

A poem scribbled in the phone notes of an exhausted healthcare
worker during COVID-19.

Let us lament for one more patient gone.
No time to grieve this relentless monsoon;
Patience waxing and waning for the dawn.

When palpable is my heart's wasting brawn,
Errands accosted by a maskless goon.
Let us lament for one more patient gone.

No surprise, my apparition withdrawn
For life feels like nothing but a cartoon.
Patience waxing and waning for the dawn.

It takes seemingly nothing to bring on
Hallucinations of coughing maroon.
Let us lament for one more patient gone.

Daydreaming every memory foregone,
As I resurface from nightmares immune.
Patience waxing and waning for the dawn.

And with another caffeinated yawn,
I've become apprenticed to the moon.
Let us lament for one more patient gone;
Patience waxing and waning for the dawn.

Dementia

I still eat Pocky sticks on the curb of 140th
And see your soul in my rain puddle reflection
Or the mirrors you didn't recognize yourself in at the end.
Gravitations of grief hold me fast to my bed
When I remember watching your shadow grow darker.
This cold, dark universe constantly tries to snuff out the light
But you fished around in your purse for a lighter
and started committing the most jubilant arson.

Parking lot nickels face up are still good luck.
I wish I didn't feel the rock in my shoe.

Tributaries

We once flowed
Into the same river.
Do you not still
Have your best
Nights sleep on
My side of the
River bed?
Listening to
My babbling brooks
And finding rest
As I trace our path
In the small of your back.
You quickly sold
A parcel for a dam,
Halting the vigorous
And vibrant visions
Reflected in our waters.
I will never sell a parcel
For my babbling soul.
Some of your flow
Will always be
Part of me.

Metastasis

Hair brown like the bark of an oak somewhere.
Always had one foot on sea, one foot on shore.
My eyes could not rise from her icy stare.
Like the thorn on a rose, made my tongue feel sore.

Her integrity bent like a field of reeds
When I asked why she felt she needed to go.
She scattered cancerous thoughts like seeds
As I watched my garden grow row by row.

She hated mint ChapStick, so I wore cherry.
Wearing patience and attention I did not owe.
The weight of someone's world I can no longer carry,
But you can hold my hand when you need to let go.

Our inward destination lies somewhere
Away from the cliffs to which we cling.
In a bay long past the reef of the Sirens there…
Of knowledge, but not wisdom, they sing.

In Eden

In Eden,
Nobody hid behind
Leaves until
Eve ate the apple
And Adam followed suit.
This is why women cannot be trusted.

In Eden,
The heat vaporized sweat
With a breeze as people walked
Comfortably in their skin,
Until you came along.
You told the women to cover up
And serve to be saved,
Even though the savior said
To gouge out your eyes
If something causes *you* to sin.

In Eden,
You send young people
To build poor excuses
For housing and water.
You call her poor in forced tongues,
Even though she is richer
Than we will ever be.

Dhiiga kuma dhaqaaqo?
Somali for: Can you not feel your blood move [when you see injustice]?

The Last Supper

The poem I actually wrote
About you will never
Be read by anyone.
You did not offer me
The same honor.
The poem is called
"The Last Supper"
And the blaspheme
Comforts me when
I think about how
The last time I ate
At my favorite pho place
Before they changed the menu
Was with you.

I asked you to not
Touch two things:
My friendships
And me.

Goodbyes need not
Involve turning your
Back on people you
Tried not to love.

Elegies over Berries

The woman I was yesterday stares
Back at me in the mascara stains
Of the tissues on my kitchen chairs.
They say when it pours, it rains.

My only respite is found in the light of
The fridge; it shines on my pack
Of blueberries, which taste like love.
I let the dread roll off my back.

I like to sit silently in libraries
As tears power wash the parquet.
Cheers and elegies over berries
For the woman I was yesterday.

Art a la Carte

The kids are all grown
And surveying the arches.
Golden, not sandstone,
Sugar, grease, and starches.

Refined art a la carte.
Fascination is fleeting.
Preservation is ugly.
Art is for eating.

Reconstruction

A response to being told my faith needed "reconstruction."

Deceitful zealots are my bane.
Do not tell me I have reconstruction to do.
The Carpenter builds me up again.

From true love I will not abstain.
She holds my hand while in the pew.
Deceitful zealots are my bane.

Egocentric eisegesis is quite vain.
Hateful rhetoric they will spew.
The Carpenter builds me up again.

Righteousness is easy to feign;
Hidden in promises of a life anew.
Deceitful zealots are my bane.

From my face, all the blood may drain.
Light is disappearing, changing my hue,
But The Carpenter builds me up again.

All blood poured out with no stain.
To the bigots we bid adieu.
Deceitful zealots are my bane.
The Carpenter builds me up again.

Hebel | הֶבֶל

(advb.) something transitory or empty
(n.) vapor, breath, or vanity

You see, I can quench internal feuds
And have witnesses say I had grinned
As I lay hands on my own wounds
And whisper, "Must have been the wind."

Tired of being called temperamental
When compared to domesticated pearls.
It is fruitless to sugarcoat gentle
As you seek perfection from temporal whirls?

Evenings of kindhearted stabbing.
Do you not long for bonds eternal?
Would we not all trade candlelit gabbing
For ventures worth writing in a journal?

A redeeming light in ephemeral eyes.
A relentless aversion to sacrifices.
Why should I waste breath or pray to revise
When words are futile devices?

Perhaps I am too sentimental?
Each moment purely coincidental.

L'esprit De L'escalier

French for 'staircase wit': the predicament of
thinking of the perfect reply too late.

I found someone unconscious
In the basement shower
Drenched, but in a way
I chose to never know.

Blood is thicker than water,
But alcohol is twice as pungent.

Sometimes I still see her downtown
Under polka dot umbrellas
Adeptly avoiding the puddles
Created by my nine-year old eyes.

While taking a shower at seventeen,
I realized exactly what I should have said.

SOCIAL GRAMMAR

i am e but your I always goes before me even after c-ing
unconditional love from me

initiative put the i before we can even comprehend to begin
because you could never care enough to half ass half the hassle

momma always told me to sieze the day and if i want things done
right i better do them myself and niether time i put myself on the
line and felt the pain in my vayns did i see any sufficeint change in
heart

I before e except after seeing why you left me so out of love because
you were so broken hearted you had nothing left to give

it's always I before e and now i c y

Brittle

A daily dry baptism
With unholy dry shampoo.
I dip my head into the salt
In the wounds of the sides of you.

Many were raised on a Jesus
who was white and prestigious.
Nobody is inherently a better man.
It's okay to be the drugstore brand.

I don't wanna grow too old.
Should I smoke just in case?
Forgive my statement, bold.
Minds should not go to waste.

Bones brittle like my toffee.
My heart is thin and weary.
Secretly bitter like my coffee,
I bear a disposition cheery.

Ξενία

(xen-ee-ah)

hospitality

Love Letter to 'Murderapolis'

Suburban friends fumble their mugs on my porch
As a muffler bellows the song of maintenance costs.

> Feeling guilt as my rent bill sings of gentrification costs.
> Drink every time the neighbor says, "It's a scorcher!"

Drunken giggles in a roast, urging them to "scorch her!"
My first time finding safety in a misunderstanding.

> Newscasts of my city quaver misunderstanding.
> This was Prince's favorite city for a reason.

All my neighbors are here for a reason.
Yet we cannot find ways to house them?

> When they are hurt, I cannot call 911 for them;
> My friends are criminalized for their existence.

Not afraid to be criminalized for peaceful resistance.
I invite all kinds of relatives to sit on my porch.

There will never be anyone richer than the greens
in the East Phillips Community Garden.

Genesis 19:2

May I wash the dirt from your feet?
Lest they know you are a guest.
For if they knew, it is you they would beat,
As the dirt on your sandals is a test.

Anything I can do to make you at ease?
I will bake you bread without leaven.
For you, my guest, I would part the seas
To make my home on Earth as it is in Heaven.

Hospitalidad en La Paz

La comida transmite amor,
Mientras las tías sirven platos calientes.
Ellas me pellizcan cariñosamente
Y me llaman 'gringa flaca.'

Mientras las tías sirven platos calientes,
Niños comen con una sonrisa
Y me llaman 'gringa flaca.'
Aquí, me siento querida.

Niños comen con una sonrisa
Y ellos me pellizcan cariñosamente.
Aquí, me siento querida.
La comida transmite amor.

Hospitality in La Paz, Bolivia
A reflection on my time with the Coptic Church in rural Bolivia.

The food conveys love,
As the aunties serve hot plates.
They pinch my arm lovingly
And call me 'gringa flaca.'

As the aunties serve hot plates,
Children eat with a smile
And call me 'gringa flaca.'
Here, I feel wanted.

Children eat with a smile
And they pinch me lovingly.
Here, I feel wanted.
The food conveys love.

Appendix

I've always wondered what the artist was thinking when reading creative writing or looking at visual art. I let you, the reader, relate however you please to most of these poems without additional context. However, I have included additional details about various poems here in case you're curious.

Acknowledgements

Gittu to my family for raising me to be a curious and conscientious person. You fostered my fascination with the world and languages.
Gittu to the talented Carlos Fernandes II for writing a lovely foreword. I highly recommend his collections, *The View Within Me* and *Casually Extravagant*. It is so delightful to experience mutual support and encouragement, especially through his Juniper Tree Poetry collective.
Gittu to Minnesota author, Ben Kyriagis. Hailing from Greece with one excellent publication under his belt, he provided constructive feedback and assistance with my Greek pronunciation. I highly recommend *Don't Marry an American* which is about his hometown, journey to America, and falling in love.
Giitu to Keely and The Rush Artist for the proofread and notes. I dream of helping you publish your own exquisite poetry someday.
All praise to the bassi voiɲa (Northern Sámi for Holy Spirit) who moves through all things, including pens and paper.
Giitu, *wopida*, and *miigwech* to the Dakota, Ojibwe, and Anishinaabe peoples for their kinship and shared love for the occupied land I call home: *Mni Sota Makoce*.

Philautia: self-love

Poems about loving oneself and one's surroundings.

Ode to Obscured Ancestors

I wrote this poem seven years ago for a contest at my college where the theme was ancestry. My grandma would make remarks about how she felt empowered to do something because "We're Norskis, ya know?" When I was in middle school, an extended family member found out that our lineage is Sámi. As a result, I took interest in learning more about our history and language by making internet friends who still live in Sápmi, which spans the top of what we call Norway, Sweden, Finland, and the Kola Peninsula of Russia. We have twelve languages, three of which are extinct and nine are UNESCO endangered languages, some with less than fifty native speakers remaining. Northern Sámi, which I have slowly learned since middle school (so my translations are almost certainly not perfect), is the most common language and the language that my ancestors spoke before they were forbidden to use it in Norway or came to America identifying as Norwegian. If you'd like to learn more about us, Sofia Jannok is a prominent Sámi musician who has a TED talk called *Our Rights to Earth and Freedom* where she speaks eloquently about how environmental issues are inherently Indigenous issues, as native peoples are responsible for protecting 80% of the world's biodiversity despite being only 5% of the global population. She partnered with Bon Iver to interpret his song *8 (circle),* which is fun because he is so local that he was born between Ojibwe and Dakota lands. I know he is a Norski too because I used to date one of his cousins. Lastly, I implore you to learn more about the language, history, and rights to Earth and freedom of the people whose land we call home in the Midwest.

A Primer for Eluding Death by Cave Dweller
This is a four-part Duplex-style poem engaging with the process of 'enlightenment' from the perspective of a prisoner in Plato's infamous *Allegory of the Cave*. This poem is a commentary on how society sometimes shows extreme disdain toward evolving one's perspectives and opinions based on new evidence or learning. It was written in the wake of the COVID-19 pandemic based on my experience as a budding scientist and healthcare worker witnessing resistance and distrust toward the scientific community. Duplex is one of my favorite poem structures. It was masterfully invented by Jericho Brown. I highly recommend his Pulitzer Prize-winning book *The Tradition*.

The Perennial Purpose
I originally wrote this with the intention of creating something to empower my ex who struggles with Catholic guilt. In the past, both of us have sourced self-worth from our usefulness to other people

and how helpful we can be. We are human beings, not human doings. There is inherent worth in every human being.

In Another Time
This is one of three poems in this book inspired by the ancient poet, Sappho. The italicized lines at the end are a direct quote. From 1920 to 2020, this poem outlines one-hundred years of queer history with many historical references.

The first stanza embodies ballroom culture, which first emerged during the Harlem Renaissance. The Ballroom Scene is a Black and Latine underground 2SLGBTQ+ subculture originating in late 20th century New York City in response to racist experiences in established drag pageant circuits. Many popular dance moves, slang terms, fashion trends, and musical innovations were appropriated from ball culture over the past century. Vogueing and language found in the popular *RuPaul's Drag Race* originate from ball culture. RuPaul's structure is built around the traditional ball format. The television show *Pose* is a great place to learn about this history.

The second stanza juxtaposes modern summer pride parades and their sparkly, DIY joy with the harrowing history of how queer people were treated during WWII by both the Nazis and the allied forces. Queer Jewish people were forced to wear pink triangles to be easily identified and targeted. The war ended faster due to the brilliant work of a queer mathematician, Alan Turing. He cracked the Enigma code to understand Nazi strategy. This allowed for the forces to defeat them several years faster than it may have taken otherwise. This genius action saved thousands of lives and built part of the foundation for modern computers. Unfortunately, Alan Turing died from cyanide poisoning after life became unbearable due to the chemical castration punishment set by the English government for being gay. Queerness was not legal in England until 1967.

Before being called AIDS (acquired immunodeficiency syndrome), stage 3 HIV was called GRID (gay-related immune deficiency). ACT UP (AIDS Coalition to Unleash Power) was founded in New York City in 1987 as a political action group to end the AIDS pandemic and to combat the extreme homophobia resulting from stigma and stereotypes. The reference to adoption relates to the lasting difficulty for queer couples to adopt or foster children despite the large number of children in need of loving, supportive families. Legislation continues to harm queer couples and children; marriage equality and decriminalization are not enough.

Don't Ask, Don't Tell was a US military policy from 1994 to 2011 prohibiting military personnel from discriminating against or harassing closeted queer service members or applicants, while barring openly queer people from service. Our presence was deemed "an unacceptable risk to the high standards of morale, good order, discipline, and unit cohesion that are the essence of military capability."

This poem was written four years after the Pulse shooting and during the aftermath of the murder of George Floyd in our beloved city of Minneapolis. The entire world looked toward us as we imploded with righteous outrage. He lived in my friend's neighborhood. People came from outside the city to riot for the sake of rioting rather than protesting the murder of a community member at the hands of police.

Masked groups were suspiciously photographed placing bricks in non-construction areas to give the masses more means to destroy in the name of George Floyd. This concerned community organizers as this fueled a global narrative to demonize our city. At the time, I was working in a pharmacy just outside the city. Several of the destroyed buildings were chain or family-owned pharmacies, so we spent several days with three times our normal staff, transferring prescriptions for impacted community members. During this, I was meditating on how the first pride parade was a riot against police brutality led by community leaders such as Marsha P. Johnson, where bricks were thrown in self-defense. Many of our patients were understandably scared and frustrated as their prescriptions were delayed. One of the most patient people during this time was an elderly Black woman who would have been a teenager during the civil rights movement. I spent my shift praying for her safety emotionally and physically, as she has spent a lifetime watching people get brutalized at the hands of the community or the state and experiencing the consequences of racism.

The poem ends with that iconic line from Sappho, as we must never forget the actions of those whose shoulders we stand upon to continue seeking justice.

Battlefield
This poem is about my experience having audio-color synesthesia and memories of feeling overstimulated in middle school computer labs.

Kairos
To be honest, I wrote this when I was fifteen and I have no idea what it is about other than I enjoy the age-old midwestern tradition of watching storms with my dad. I submitted it to contests when I had nothing better to submit and it was an honorable mention several times, so I thought it was worth including here even though I find it to be mediocre. My experiences submitting to writing contests where my worst stuff won awards sent me into a phase where I vowed to "write badly because that's what people like these days." What a twerp I was!

Philia: fondness
Poems about friendship and affinity.

Buorre Beaivvi, Hnub Ci
One of my closest coworkers is named Hnub Ci (English spelling: Nouchi. "New-key." Rhymes with spooky.) Her name is Hmong for *sunshine*. With my interest in languages, life goal of learning a tonal language, and my love for Minnesota, I once began learning Hmong. In Minnesota, both Hmong and Sámi have the largest populations in the world outside of their ancestral homelands. However, I started to focus on learning Somali because far more people need interpreters for Somali than Hmong in Minnesota. One of our favorite things to say is "Good morning!' to patients because the phrase represents a new day and a fresh start. In Northern Sámi, we say *Buorre beaivvi* meaning "Good sun!" I am glad that the Universe gave me Hnub Ci, my sunshine-filled friend.
I'll conclude with my favorite stories learned in Hmong to illustrate the difficulty of tonal languages for people who did not grow up

speaking one. *Kuv pauv* means "I exchanged" and sounds like *Kuv tso paus* to an untrained ear. I know this because of a story where a student accidentally said *Kuv tso paus*, "I farted," in class.

Vessels
This poem represents how we often expect each other or ourselves to carry the emotions and experiences of others, allowing them to make homes and live rent-free in our hearts. I like to think of humans as vessels or conduits to help each other get to shore, but we cannot become houseboats to host the emotions of others. If our hearts get too heavy and exceed capacity, we will sink.

The Cedar
I attended a PWI Swedish Baptist college where I was told I was "too white" to lead our Indigenous student group. This was despite having the backing of the largely Indigenous Black Student Union. I wanted to use the funding to bring Dakota leaders onto campus to educate and engage our student body. Being called too white by this institution is amusing because the founders of the school were of a demographic that burned my ancestors at the stake, accusing them of devil worship for singing *joik*. My friend, who is Métis and the subject of this poem, ended up restarting the student group and did an excellent job even though there were only five of us.

Letter to an Old Dog
This poem is about a dog named Zoe who passed away shortly after I wrote the poem. I was able to dog sit for her one last time near her sixteenth birthday. I watched her so often as a kid that she functionally felt like my first dog.

The Bus from Abingdon
When I studied in Oxford in 2019, I became close friends with a random British guy at climbing practice because I asked him for beta, and we had good banter. I would often go to Stewart's apartment after practice to cook dinner and hang out. I was a science student at a Christian Humanities study abroad program, and he was a "flaming atheist" engineer. Despite our differences, we were kindred spirits. I came out as queer at Oxford when I read more into liberation theology and better understood my religion in

the context of gender and sexuality studies. The cold December nights walking outside Stewart's building and seeing my breath were reminiscent of Minnesota. The reference to keeping books warm is a nod to how the Bodleian library keeps books underneath cobblestone streets for storage.

Weeds on the Playground
This pantoum is for my friend Maria whom I met at five years old on a soccer team. We were far more interested in picking dandelions and gabbing than playing defense. She balances being a child at heart with being a wise old soul. I am deeply grateful for her.

Yoko Meshi
Growing up a teacher's child, I was obsessed with learning fun facts like words that are hard to translate between languages. As someone who loves to know a little of a lot of languages but is only colloquially functional in three, this noun struck me. Communicating in Northern Sámi feels exactly like eating a messy meal and have words fall out of my mouth.

Chess for Creatives
I have been known to call rock climbing "chess for people like me who cannot sit still."

Søndag
I have always felt closest to God in nature and try to get outside to pray at least once per Sunday. I wrote this in my head while camping at Tettegouche on an October Sunday while admiring how the conifers were boldly green amongst the lovely orange and maroon leaves.

Erototropia: flirtation
Poems for crushes and such.

Wish You Were Here & The Knowing
I wrote these poems in the wake of getting to know a witty and compassionate woman in Chicago over FaceTime and visits

between Chicago and Minneapolis until I move. I feel like the poems about what I want in a long-term relationship, like *Rose Thorn Crowns*, were written about a person of her character.

Whirlpool
This fall, I will have been out as queer for five years. I have dated some incredible people, but sometimes dating feels like trying to swim out of a whirlpool. On the line about never going to school for poetry, I learned everything I know by surrounding myself with people who are smarter writers than I am. That's why I'm passionate about making book publishing and other creative resources accessible to the public.

Sonnet for my Local Drive-In
Drive-in movies are a staple for summer entertainment in Minnesota. This is based on the kind of date that my hopeless romantic high school self would have loved to go on.

Misplaced Redame
As mentioned in the preface, this poem is about someone sitting in a library because she is in love with the librarian. To pass the time, she decides to read the dictionary. This poem is the result of her learning obscure words and being upset by the fact that the librarian has a budding relationship.

Analgesic for Growing Pains
Although it's clear that this poem is about summer romance, there is a fun story to go with this one. In the summer after college, I dated a naturalist named Sally. It was a magical summer. We shared many of the same values but did not relate on a spiritual level. I wrote to my favorite podcast, Under Our Roof, which consists of a sapphic married couple talking about life. They ask for "queeries" where many of the questions regard relationships or spirituality. Since the sapphic Christian dating pool is small, I wondered if I should continue seeing Sally as a positive dating experience or if I should try to find someone who I could see myself dating long-term even though I had applied to move to Norway. I ended up meeting my then partner shortly after Sally ended things. My former long-term girlfriend became a fan of the podcast and

asked if that anonymous question was submitted by me because it "sounded like your writing." This was only four months after we met! Nearly three years later, I remain pals with Sally and am pursuing friendship with my ex. Regarding the drawing, I like the accidental imagery of two peas in a pod with us in the hammock. In real life, my hair does not look like ramen, and I am not built like a linebacker.

Yesterday Morning
This pantoum represents how I tend to talk in circles during stimulating conversations and must walk back to the original point of the subject.

Eros: desire
Poems for longing, desire, and lost love.

Green for your Eyes
I wrote this in Oxford after a friend told me that she was reading *Sir Gawain and the Green Knight*. I felt inspired by how green represented honor, and I was struggling with my ex getting into a new relationship instead of trying long-distance with me. I knew that the more honorable thing to do was to keep my feelings inside and not express them. The green carnation is a nod to Oscar Wilde.

From Stardust
This poem is about the same person discussed above and was written during the same period. He was the last man I dated before coming out as queer, which is what the line about "Hebrew renders depth I never shared" is about.

Argon
I asked a girl in my night class (who I thought was flirting with me) to watch a meteor shower. One week, she was gone when I was wearing a fabulous outfit that her roommate commented positively on. When she returned, she remarked, "I heard you looked like Harry Styles last week, bummer I missed it!" Why am I a topic of conversation at home? It turns out, she had a devoted boyfriend, now husband. In my defense, the alleged flirtatious comments were…intriguing. We never went to watch the meteor shower as

friends, but this poem was written as if things worked out how I imagined they would, had things been romantic.

Calamitous Consonants
I wrote this when I was fifteen and I genuinely have no idea who it is about.

Boulevard of Broken Pens
I would describe this poem as prophetic because I wrote it right before my now ex unexpectedly dumped me before I moved to Chicago for medical school. I wrote many poems in response to the breakup, most of which I kept to myself.

Pragma: Enduring love
Poems for lasting, fulfilling romantic relationships.

Rose Thorn Crowns
This poem is part of a series of three that was inspired by quotes from Sappho, all of which end with the quote in italics. The other two are *In Another Time* and *Gentile*. This poem uses the Biblical euphemism of "knowing" someone intimately to deconstruct the sexualization of sapphic relationships in popular culture. This describes the emotional intimacy of a sapphic relationship juxtaposed with the narrator's relationship with Jesus. The end is meant to mean multiple things but was inspired by imagery of Jesus as the bridegroom and disciples as the wedding guests. To me, the ending Sappho line here is imagery of walking down the aisle to see the love of your life as led by Christ. It is intentionally vague for interpretation by the reader.
The queer history references are the use of violets and green carnations (look up green carnations and Oscar Wilde) to signal queerness. "To dance among the righteous in fields of green carnations" is a reference to queer solidarity amongst persecuted identities like trans and Two Spirit individuals. The faithful centurion in the Gospels of Matthew and Luke is thought by some scholars to be a gay man. Daniel Helminiak, Tat-Siong Benny Liew, and Theodore Jennings Jr. are some of the Christian authors who

uphold the idea that the word *pais* used for the servant could have the undertone of a lover based on Roman historical data about patron-client relationships. Jesus did not condemn them and healed them without concern for this potential dynamic.

The title is a nod to Jesus' crown of thorns and the common gift of roses without thorns in romantic relationships. I love braiding and making flower crowns for people.

U-Haul
This poem is about a fulfilling relationship that was mutually perceived as something that would end in marriage. Though that relationship came to an end, I now hold these hopes for a new potential person in my life. The image is from Freepik.com by @starline with a free license and required attribution.

Feeling Wholly
I adore Norwegian idioms. This poem was written for partners whom I have said *jeg er glad i deg* to. I wanted to write a villanelle (my favorite form) about the difference between *jeg elsker deg* (I love you) and *jeg er glad i deg* (I am fond of you.) *Jeg er glad i deg* is often said to close friends, partners, and loved ones on occasion. It is very Norski to show love through action rather than words. *Jeg elsker deg* is said very earnestly and infrequently to family and partners. I have only said it to family, and I will probably only say it to a partner if I get married. Since this book explores concepts of love in various languages, this was the perfect piece to include. Growing up, there was a subculture for Norwegian-Americans of not verbalizing emotions that I subverted as a child. My other Norski friends like to joke about how we are inadvertently taught to not talk about our emotions. I was the first person to get my extended family to regularly say *I love you* to family members.

A Joik for my Love
Joik is a traditional Sámi song without words that is meant to encapsulate a person, a place, a memory, nature, an animal, etcetera. Sometimes words can be interspersed throughout, but it is mostly vocalizations. Historically, this part of our culture is something I have kept to myself. This poem is about the first person I would joik as prayer in front of.

Simultaneous

This was written for an ex who intended on marrying me someday but broke up with me out of fear of the future and doing long distance to Chicago. I am grateful for the time we spent together and the things we taught each other.

First Lady

This was written about the same relationship above in a Kwik Trip since I thought of it while driving. I was the first woman she ever dated, and she had an uncanny ability to recall facts about famous First Ladies.

Storge: familial love

Poems for family, for better or worse.

Blood and Chosen

These sister poems were written about the phrase "Blood of the covenant is thicker than the water of the womb" indicating that some chosen family bonds are stronger than blood relative bonds. I am lucky to have both close blood and chosen family bonds.

They Dance with Me

We grew up as a mac and cheese and pizza family due to busy sports schedules and my parents' disinterest in cooking other than on special occasions. My mom is a 4th grade teacher and pours her heart and soul into her work. I am exceptionally proud of my family.

My brother is an excellent singer and self-taught guitarist. My dad can also sing well, but he is better at his job as a "professional hype man" where his leadership role is focused on uplifting employees to be the best they can be.

My mom has always been a little envious that I got the thicker, wavy/curly hair of my dad's family. My grandma taught me how to do basic braids and I taught myself how to do things like five strand braids. Nonetheless, these women wove their courage into me.

My dad is bad at putting on sunscreen but surprisingly rarely burns. I am the same way. I like to joke that it is because our ancestors are from the land of the midnight sun. My mom is a very independent person and likes to do most things herself. She puts a lot of weight and responsibility on her own shoulders instead of asking us to share responsibility for tasks. We have worked on being proactive in asking her how we can support her.

My dad has a hard time with conflict for personal reasons. Due to this, I try to rarely argue with him. I've spent my career defending my intelligence to men as a woman in STEM who was assaulted by a classmate in college. This is why I "bark" at men with good intentions in conversations and become easily defensive. My analogy is based on rescue dogs that I've cared for as a dog sitter who react differently to my masculine friends.

The Lightest Reindeer Calf
The title is inspired by a song called *Čuoivvatmiessi* by Sofia Jannok. I wrote this fictional story loosely based on themes of family with my experience in Sápmi in 2019.

Agape: love for humanity, love from God
Poems about loving humanity and nature either from the perspective of creation or the Creator.

Liturgy of the Ordinary
This poem is about the rhythm and beauty found in everyday life. I thank Robin Wall Kimmerer for my obsession with moss and lichen. Check out her bryology episode on Ologies podcast.

She Sings
This poem is inspired by themes of the ethereal beauty of mornings, God as a mother, the execution of Jesus, and how I love when people who "can't sing" sing passionately. There is another reference to the Norwegian tradition of walking in nature on Sundays called Søndag.

Helium
This poem is part of my *Periodical* series personifying the periodic table. It is about a fictional ten-year-old girl watching Apollo 11 launch on her birthday. She grew up to love astrophysics and math. Her parents worried about misogyny in aerospace engineering and wanted the best for their daughter while being concerned for her. Her grandpa was a war veteran who unequivocally believed in her.

Gentile
This is the third poem in the Sappho series where the end line is a Sappho quote. Gentiles were seen as outsiders in the Hebrew Bible and disciples sought reconciliation with them. This is about the ambiguity toward queer identities in many churches and unwelcoming stances of "we welcome you, but we don't agree with your existence."

Sounds of Rounds with the Patient Care Philharmonic
A friend made a fun game of personifying medical specialties as musical instruments. This is a rondeau about physicians rounding on and intervening in the life of a patient throughout the lifespan, ending with palliative care ("malleative care.")

The Blessing of the Sun, the River, and the Moon
This was written as I laid on the banks of the Mississippi river. I used to live right next to a trail and access point. I would watch the sun set and the stars come out. I would watch the University of Minnesota rowing team chant down the river as I tried to read Mary Oliver.

My Sister, Mary Oliver
This short story is based on true stories about my brother's birth and my trip to Sápmi in 2019. It is inspired by the poetry and essays of Mary Oliver.

The Nomadic Ways of Wildflowers and Weeds
I wrote this in response to a prompt for National Poetry Writing Month. It was inspired by my friend Keely who is a naturalist and does a brilliant job representing the world through her poetry and

how she personifies birds when we watch them. She taught me that I resonate with the American coot.

There is a reference to how the Spanish missionaries spread yellow mustard seed to trace their paths with symbolizing the parable of the mustard seed. It is invasive.

Third Fig

I wrote this after getting the tattoo featured on the same page as the poem. It is based on *First Fig* and *Second Fig* by Edna St. Vincent Millay, which I will include below. I love figures of botanical drawings, so I got figs to represent rebirth. Wasps must enter the female fig to pollinate it, but the wasp cannot lay eggs and consequently dies. The fig produces an enzyme that digest the wasp entirely. The crunchy bits are seeds, not wasp.

First Fig
My candle burns at both ends;
*   It will not last the night;*
But ah my foes, and oh my friends –
*   It gives a lovely light!*

Second Fig
Safe upon the solid rock the ugly houses stand:
Come and see my shining palace build upon the sand!

Thrínos: lament
Poems for somber times, where sitting with feelings is a form of love.

Longing for a New Moon
This villanelle was written when I was working overtime giving COVID-19 and flu shots to immunocompromised people as a pharmacy technician. It was beyond exhausting, but I was glad to serve my community. I respect people's autonomy, but it was disheartening to be asked by anti-maskers why I was wearing an N95 in public.

Dementia

My paternal grandmother died from dementia. I am like her in many ways and was very close to her. This poem is about my relationship with her near death and after death, as I would mourn the loss by sitting outside the convenience store that we would walk to and get Pocky Sticks at when I was a child. She told me that finding coins face up is good luck, even if they aren't pennies. Grief feels like a rock in my shoe. It is always there and hard to ignore. It is possible for our brains to learn to ignore the sensation, but it takes a lot of mental gymnastics.

Tributaries

I was broken up with around the time I saw the exceptional documentary *Bad River* about how the Bad River reservation saved Lake Superior from disastrous oil spills using their land autonomy and refusing to sell land parcels. I used imagery of rivers and dams to demonstrate my feelings about the abrupt breakup. It made me think of Runeard's Dam in my favorite movie of all time: *Frozen II*. The Northuldra people represent Sámi, and they were successful in breaking it with Anna and Elsa. I will not sell out to halt the flow of my spirit.

In Eden

As a basic Somali learner, this is one of my favorite poems in this book. I love the phrase posing the question of whether one can feel their blood coursing through their body when they see injustice. This poem is about Africa being colonized in the name of Christianity and the deep sin and injustice that worked to dehumanize and erase cultures. It finishes with the misconception that Africa is full of "poor" people, so it is commonly visited for mission trips. Sometimes international cultural exchange can be positive, but I have heard too many horror stories of inexperienced outsiders spending thousands to come to foreign countries to try to build infrastructure that needs to be redone and repaired by local people. It is more often a burden than a blessing. Long-term international collaboration is often ethical, short-term missions often perpetuate colonialism.

Please draw your attention to the current injustices occurring in Sudan and the Congo and how our consumption of technology and need for mining impact the rich natural resources and people of African countries.

The Last Supper & Metastasis
These are composites. Pretty clear storytelling and world building based on relationships with two different people who hurt me. I wish them the best.

Elegies over Berries
This poem is about feeling depressed and finding joy in the small things like fresh blueberries. It carries themes of learning about oneself and letting the old self die to become anew when rising from a difficult period of life.

Art a la Carte
This poem has nothing to do with distaste toward an institution that rhymes with Nick Schmonalds, allegedly, and the fact that people deserve better access to healthy food. It merely explores the shift in childhoods from exploring natural structures like sandstone to living in artificial environments.

Reconstruction
My response to a college friend telling me that my faith had "some reconstruction yet to do," because I believe that queer marriage and trans identities are affirmed by the Bible and he does not.

Hebel
This is written about the same tumultuous relationship as *From Stardust* and *Green for your Eyes*. I had a scarcity mindset and feared not being able to find someone who was a good match for me. I was wrong!
My love for the word *hebel* stems from the Vapor meditation by The Liturgists, which is a liturgy based on the teachings of *Kohelet* in Ecclesiates about the vapor of all things.

L'Esprit D'Escalier
This poem is about things I wish I had said to someone who caused emotional turmoil but I was too young to know what to say to them.

SOCIAL GRAMMAR
This was inspired by my childhood love for E.E. Cummings, the grammar rebel. Queer people can often relate to having a deep friendship that inexplicably blows up in your face and then later realizing it was homoerotic but neither of you were out yet. That is what this was about. I had a close friend who hurt me interpersonally and in relationships with our mutual friends because of her jealousy.

Brittle
I'm not sure what to tell you, dear reader, about this one other than that I was feeling similarly to how Sufjan Stevens does in his song *America* where he explores his distaste with Americanized Christianity. Read the lyrics for an interesting reflection if this one resonated with you.

Xenia: hospitality
Poems for radically welcoming others as an extension of love.

Love letter to 'Murderapolis'
One of my favorite living situations was subleasing as a recent college grad from a college student and her four roommates on the University of Minnesota campus. However, we lived on a bad block of Dinkytown where there were up to three armed carjackings on our block in one week. Despite this, I absolutely adored living there and felt generally safe. This was after the global news dubbed our city 'Murderapolis' without actually addressing the nuance of living in different areas of such a big city. Friends from the suburbs were scared to come to my apartment even in the daytime. In another area of Minneapolis that I lived in, there was a large unhoused population. Several of my unhoused neighbors would hang out by our local Aldi and I got to know them a bit. Some of them were diabetic and helped me to realize my groceries contained a lot of sugar. I was involved with protests to protect the local encampments

from eviction because all it does, usually, is escalate situations by making it harder for social workers to find their clients. Not having a place to sleep further criminalizes their existence, raising crime instead of preventing it by dissolving effective encampments. My favorite protest was providing supplies to people resisting the demolition of the Depot in East Phillips. Phillips is a neighborhood impacted by redlining and environmental racism. Constructing on the Depot site would have released a large amount of arsenic into the environment, and the city was not listening to community proposals about turning the building into a yearlong community garden instead of destroying the building. The protest worked, and the garden will open to the public soon.

Genesis 19:02
This poem is about radical hospitality and the misunderstanding of Genesis 19 that leads to condemnation of queer people when one does not consider historical dispositions towards outsiders in ancient Middle Eastern culture. Two angels visit Lot and he tells them to shake and wash the dirt from their sandals so that the people of Sodom would be less likely to recognize them as new arrivals to his home.
Lot instructs the angels to stay inside, lest they be persecuted as foreigners. He made them a meal, including bread without leaven. Before bed, all the men from Sodom surrounded the house to gang rape the angels, which was unfortunately not an uncommon unfriendly welcome to outsiders. Lot offers his two virgin daughters to be raped and the men try to break down his door to get to the angels. The angels pull lot inside and make the men of Sodom blind so they cannot find the door. Lot instructs his family to leave Sodom since the Lord will destroy it.
Jesus says in Ezekiel 16 that the sin of Sodom was selfishness, haughtiness and arrogance, "Now this was the sin of your sister Sodom: She and her daughters were arrogant, overfed, and unconcerned; they did not help the poor and needy. They were haughty and did detestable things before me. Therefore, the Lord did away with them as you have seen." Some people view the "detestable things" as homosexual lust instead of gang rape and assault, which was far more common. Unfortunately, this has

caused some Christians to become hostile towards queer people, when the intent of the passage was radical hospitality.

Hospitalidad en La Paz

I was invited by the Coptic Medical Association of North America to translate for their childhood health education program in rural Bolivia in 2017. Most of the other Americans who were Egyptian were mistaken for Latine, so I had to teach them how to tell people to come talk to me. The monks only spoke Arabic and Spanish, so our group conversations were in Arabic and people had to interpret for me even though I was there as the interpreter. My Spanish was far better back then as I tested out of collegiate Spanish. I am excited to take advanced Spanish in medical school here soon. My time in Bolivia helped me to understand true hospitality, as I was an outsider to both Coptic and Bolivian cultures despite my knowledge of their languages and histories.

Let's finish with a preview of my next book, *The Periodical*. *Helium* and *Argon* will also appear in *The Periodical*.

The Periodical is a series of poetry books inspired by an interview with my hero and muse, Dr. Oliver Sacks. Dr. Sacks was an infamous neurologist and writer with a peculiar life; he was filled with childlike wonder about the periodic table. He and his partner Bill Hayes are two of the best writers I have ever read, and I love to read (Check out *Insomniac City* by Bill Hayes. I cried bittersweet tears four times). In this interview, Dr. Sacks called himself Xenon because growing up he felt like he could not bond with anyone. However, scientists found out later in his life that Xe and F *can* bond. That aligned with when he realized he was gay. I was touched by this personification. I thought, "Man, someone should write a book personifying the periodic table. I want to read that...wait I have a chemistry degree!" In the introduction, you'll learn more about why Dr. Sacks is my muse. To put it briefly, please enjoy this cheeky book personifying my favorite section of the table: noble gases and friends. Upon further reflection, Dr. Sacks truly was Xenon; he was noble, inert, and sounded out of this world.

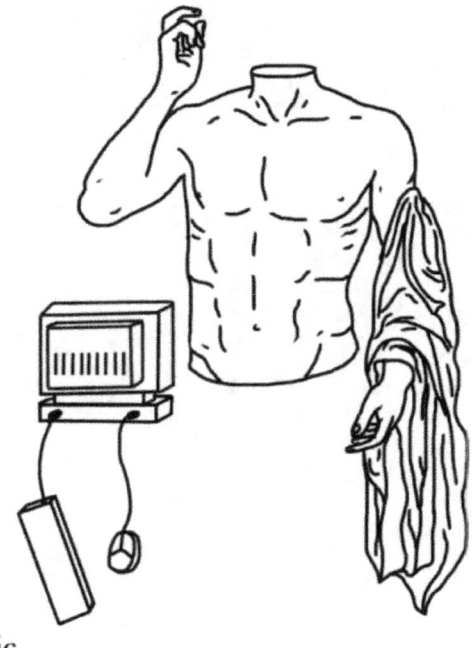

1

𝕳

Purely diatomic,
Rejoinders diabolic,
Averse to being alone.

Only treadmill is hedonic,
Elementally sardonic,
Ironically bound to the phone.

Feels heavy like deuterium.
Saturday morning delirium;
In the nimbus is a mirror.

Shelling for a premium,
Scrambling for elysium,
But the water isn't clearer.

11

www.ingramcontent.com/pod-product-compliance
Lightning Source LLC
Chambersburg PA
CBHW071203120626
46546CB00006B/2400